PEOPLE

Written by
Noda Rottridge

Illustrated by
Robert Lewis

HARRAP

Contents

Population	4
The Human Body	6
Cultures	8
Amazing Feats	10
Records	12
Language and Communication	14
Food	16
Money	18
Inventions and Discoveries	20
Royalty and Rulers	22
Warfare	24
Superstitions	26
Myths and Legends	28
Facts and Fallacies	30
Index	32

First published in Great Britain 1990
by HARRAP BOOKS Ltd
Chelsea House, 26 Market Square, Bromley BR1 1NA

Produced for HARRAP BOOKS Ltd by Times Four Publishing Ltd

Text ©Times Four Publishing Ltd 1990

Artwork ©RCS Graphics Ltd 1990

All rights reserved. No part of this publication may be reproduced in any form or by any means without the prior permission of Harrap Books Ltd.

ISBN 0 245-60065-5

Colour reproduction by RCS Graphics Ltd
Typeset by Etel Computer Setting
Printed in Britain by Cambus Litho

About this book

This book is packed full of unusual and interesting facts about people. For example, did you know that around 155 babies are born every minute? In this book you can find out about...

Food
What did people eat in Roman times? They were very fond of stuffed dormice!

Communication
How many languages can you speak? There are about 5,000 different languages in the world to choose from.

Facts & Fallacies
What is a fact and what is a fallacy? For example, did the Roman Emperor Nero really ignore the fact that the city of Rome was burning down?

The Human Body
Find out facts about your body! If you grew your hair, do you think it could grow to 6 metres?

Inventions and Discoveries
Find out about bright sparks like Thomas Edison, who patented over 1,000 inventions!

Myths and Legends
A huge island called Atlantis was once said to have existed in the Atlantic Ocean and to have been destroyed by an earthquake. Find out more about myths and legends further on.

Population

Population explosion
In 8000 BC, the population was about 6 million. By 1800 AD, it had grown 159 times, to 954 million. By the 1930s it had more than doubled again. In the next 30 years the population grew yet another 1,000 million. By the year 2000 it will be about 6,122 million.

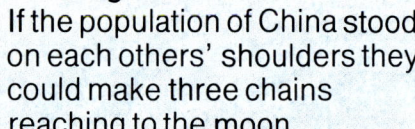

Drawing down the moon
If the population of China stood on each others' shoulders they could make three chains reaching to the moon.

Popular Places

Busy cities
The most highly populated city in the world is probably Tokyo, with around 11,903,900 citizens. Mexico City is catching up fast and is expected to expand beyond its current 10,499,000.

The quiet life
The territory with the smallest human population (but plenty of penguins) is Antartica. Since 1956, it has been permanently occupied by scientists. At times, the population swells to 2,000.

The Human Body

Lengthy locks
An Indian man may have the longest hair in the world, with locks measuring over 6m. An American woman has hair over 3m long and still growing.

Water babies
The world record for staying underwater voluntarily is 13 mins 42.5 secs. A two-year old who fell into a creek survived after being underwater for over an hour.

Ring necked
Women with the longest necks in the world are likely to be members of the Padaung or Kareni tribe of Burma. They lengthen their necks to measure up to 40cm by wearing copper rings.

Teething trouble
A dentist in Italy kept all the teeth he had taken out. When they were counted, he had over 2,000,000 teeth.

Body Facts

Growth spurt
At what age do you grow the most? Before you are born! If you carried on growing at the same rate as a baby in the last few months before you were born, you would end up being huge. You would be about 16m high by the time you were ten years old!

Inside facts
Did you know that if it were possible to take out your intestines and unravel them, they are so long they would stretch across a tennis court.

Water bodies
An adult's body is 60 per cent water! If you think that is hard to imagine, then it is probably because your brain is even wetter – it is 80 per cent water.

Hearty facts
When you are not moving around, your heart still manages to beat 100,000 times a day.

Cultures

Culture and Customs

Beliefs, customs and cultures vary in different parts of the world. What one culture considers to be normal, another may find strange.

Bull leaping
In Ancient Crete, teams of young girls and boys would vault over the horns of a charging bull. Nobody knows exactly why they did this – it may have been a religious rite.

Sneezing with soul
People say 'bless you' when you sneeze, because of an ancient belief. People thought that if you sneezed, your soul was in danger of being blown out of your nose. By saying 'bless you', it means that you hope the person's soul stays inside their body.

Time for the devil
Many cultures believe that the devil can be scared off by ringing church bells. If a church clock rings thirteen times, it is thought to be the work of the devil.

A pot of lies
Rumours that tribes in the Congo were cannibals are now thought to have been invented.

Funny money
In some areas of the South Pacific, shells or fruit can sometimes be used as money. Would you take a gamble on that?

Spartan sports
In Sparta, part of Ancient Greece, girls were brought up to be very tough. They were trained in boxing and also wrestling.

American mail
Letter writing seems to be a strong part of American culture. On average, a person living in the USA will receive nearly 600 letters a year. A letter was even sent to a mouse in the USA.

Amazing Feats

Free fall
Twenty-one year old Flight Sergeant Nicholas Alkemade, fell over 5,000m out of a blazing aeroplane, in 1944. He landed in snow over Germany and amazingly survived his long fall.

A handy feat
In 1900 an Austrian man called Johann Hurlinger, walked from Vienna to Paris, a distance of 1400km. The extraordinary thing about this walk was that he did it on his hands!

No peace from pilgrims
Saint Simeon Stylites was a Syrian monk, who lived in the desert because he wanted peace and quiet. But pilgrims still came to see him, so to get some peace he built himself a pillar 15m high and lived atop it for 45 years.

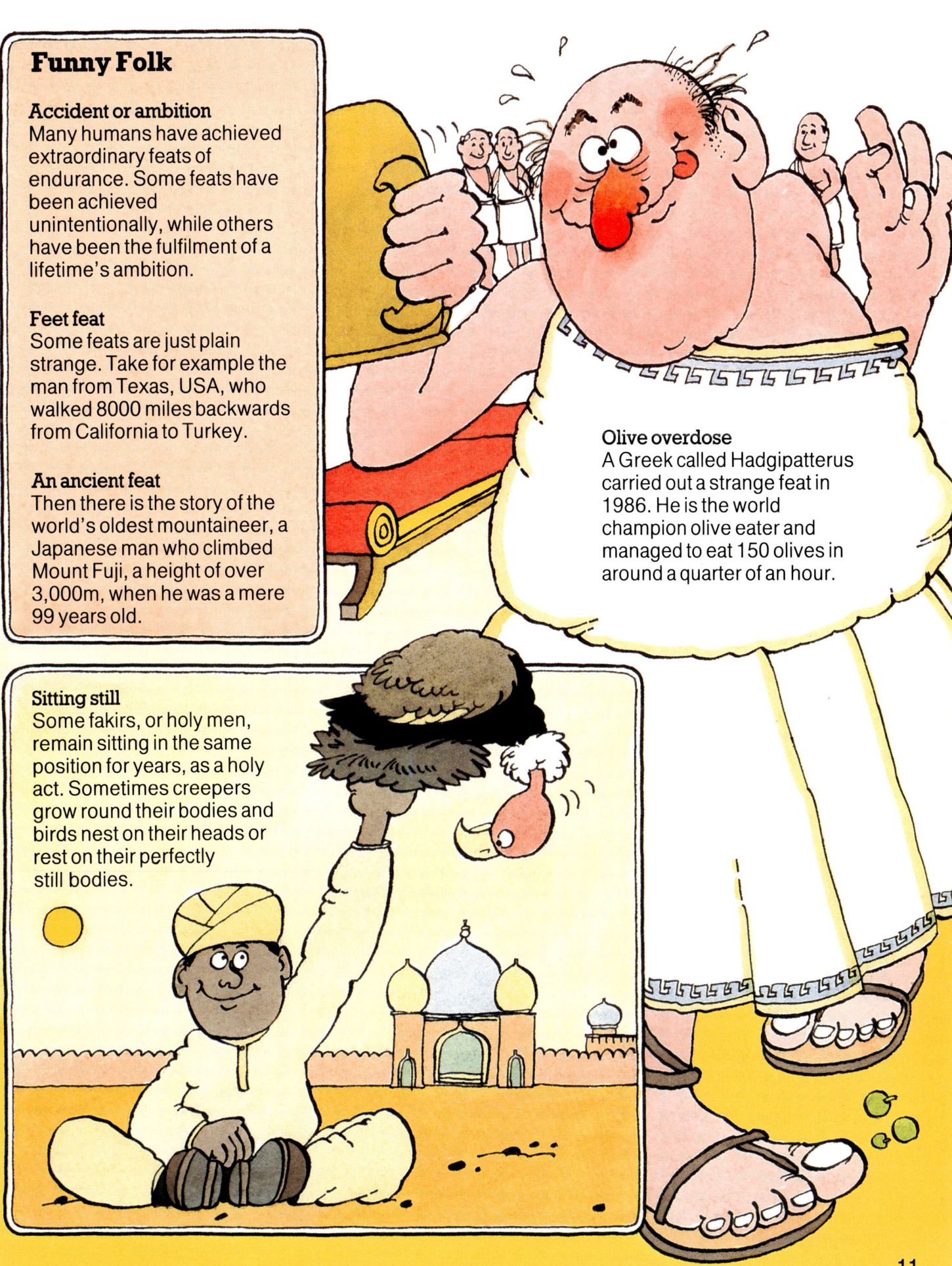

Funny Folk

Accident or ambition
Many humans have achieved extraordinary feats of endurance. Some feats have been achieved unintentionally, while others have been the fulfilment of a lifetime's ambition.

Feet feat
Some feats are just plain strange. Take for example the man from Texas, USA, who walked 8000 miles backwards from California to Turkey.

An ancient feat
Then there is the story of the world's oldest mountaineer, a Japanese man who climbed Mount Fuji, a height of over 3,000m, when he was a mere 99 years old.

Olive overdose
A Greek called Hadgipatterus carried out a strange feat in 1986. He is the world champion olive eater and managed to eat 150 olives in around a quarter of an hour.

Sitting still
Some fakirs, or holy men, remain sitting in the same position for years, as a holy act. Sometimes creepers grow round their bodies and birds nest on their heads or rest on their perfectly still bodies.

Records

The jumbo jetset
One of the largest commercial airliners in the world is the Boeing 747. It has a capacity of up to 500 passengers. In 1974, the record for the largest number of passengers carried was made when a Boeing 747 carried 674 passengers.

Strange happenings

Millions of maggots
People will do all sorts of odd things to get in the news. Peter Smart sat in a bath filled with 2 million maggots for 24 hours.

Having a whale of a time
James Bartley probably did not have any desire to make a record as the person to live the longest inside a whale. He was out with the crew of his boat when he fell overboard, into the jaws of a whale.

The next day, the same whale was harpooned. To the surprise of the crew, when they cut open the whale, they found James alive, although unconscious, in the stomach of the whale. He had been bleached white by the digestive juices of the whale.

Rejected writers
One author's manuscript has been rejected over 200 times by publishers who do not want to print it. Another man had 176 rejections in around two years.

A singular success
The youngest person to make record time sailing solo is seventeen year old David Sandeman, who is British.
  He sailed on his own from Jersey in the Channel Islands, across the Atlantic to Rhode Island, USA in 43 days.

Menu madness
The Tumpnak restaurant in Thailand probably has rather a large menu. The restaurant can hold 3,000 people and has 1000 waiters.

Dragon breath
The largest flame ever blown from someone's mouth was measured as 8.2 metres, in 1985. The thrower was a British man, Reg Morris.

Language and Communication

Talking together
There are about 5,000 languages spoken in the world today. The most commonly spoken language is Mandarin, used by 715 million Chinese.

Communication Facts

Letter lovers
Americans send the most letters in the world — around 90,000 million every year. Two British lovers sent each other 6,000 letters during 4½ years apart.

The Cardinal and Chinese
A Cardinal Mezzofanti was one of the world's earliest linguists, fluent in 26 languages at his death in 1849. Imagine if he had tried to learn Chinese. It would have been tough. He would have had to learn the 49,905 characters listed in a forty-volume Chinese dictionary.

Lengthy writing
The Sumerians, living in around 3500BC were the first people to write down their language in pictures. The Chinese still use picture symbols, called characters. If Cardinal Mezzofanti struggled with Chinese before, he will be glad to have missed the new dictionary of Chinese which contains 20 million characters.

Phoning home
In Bangladesh, 1 person in 1,000 has a telephone. In the USA, the number is 7 out of 10 people. The USA has 114,349,000 telephone lines. The largest working phone is 3.965m high with a 3.05m handset.

Language lovers
One of the most important ways in which we all communicate is by using language. You may live in a country where only one language is commonly spoken. In India, there are 845 different languages.

Television addicts
Children between the ages of 2 and 11 years watch, on average, nearly 32 hours of television every week. Around 500 million homes in the world have television.

Loud and Clear
In Ancient Greece, there was an orator called Demosthenes. He gave speeches and it was important that he could speak loudly and clearly. So he used to practice by going down to the sea, putting pebbles in his mouth and shouting above the noise of the roaring waves.

Food

Truffle hunting
Truffles are small, mushroom-like delicacies, which grow underground. People use pigs to find them, because they love eating them too. When the pig starts digging the farmer knows there are truffles.

Mice meal
In Roman times the rich enjoyed huge feasts, where they ate a lot of things which we do not eat today. Stuffed dormice were a great delicacy.

Feeling peckish?
The largest apple pie ever baked was made at Hewitts Farm in Kent, England in 1982. It was made in a dish 12m x 7m and weighed 13.66 tonnes. In 1987 in Michigan, USA, a cherry pie was baked that was 5.33m across, 66.04cm deep and weighed 11,861kg.

Fast food
If you ate a plate of pasta which was covered in a creamy sauce, it would give you the energy to run for a whole hour.

Food Facts

Funny foods
People have been known to eat all kinds of foods. Hedgehogs, humming birds in walnut shells, camels' heels and lark's tongues are just a few of them.

Food for thought
The unfair distribution of food around the world means that many people cannot afford good food.
    An average American eats 2,100g of food a day while an average Indian has 600g.

A lifetime's supply
In an average lifetime, you will probably eat your way through around 50 tonnes of food and drink 50,000 litres of liquid.

Out to lunch
Sandwiches are named after the keen gambler the Earl of Sandwich who put cold meat between bread so that he didn't have to leave his card table to eat.

Money

Making money
The Chinese invented paper money, around AD812. Paper money remains popular as it is lighter than coins to carry.

Minute money
The lightest and probably the smallest coin in the world is a Nepalese silver coin from the mid-eighteenth century. It weighs 0.0002g, so it would hardly burn a hole in your pocket!

Got change for $100,000?
The highest amount for a bank note that is still legal currency is for US $10,000. Last printed in 1944, there are only 348 left in circulation.

Money Matters

Mean with money
A certain Henrietta Green, born in 1835, is an extraordinary example of a miser. She kept over $30,000,000 in one bank. She ate cold porridge rather than wasting money heating it up. Her son had to have his leg amputated because she was not able to find him free medical attention soon enough.

She died leaving over $90 million dollars — enough to heat up a few plates of porridge.

A generous nature
Andrew Carnegie started his working life earning $1.20 a week in a factory. By the end of his life he had donated $70 million to good causes.

Cheeky cheques
A cheque can be written on any piece of paper. It is simply a command to the bank to pay someone. Some people have taken this idea to the extreme. Imagine the cashiers' surprise when a cheque walked in to the bank! The cheque had been written on the side of a cow.

A taxing task
Taxes are compulsory payments of money to a government so that they can raise money. The highest ever demand for money to be paid by an individual as tax was $336 million on the estate of the fabulously wealthy American, Howard Hughes.

Inventions and Discoveries

Bright spark
The inventions of Thomas Edison, born in 1847, include the light bulb and the phonograph. He patented more than a thousand inventions.

Clever cleaners
The first vacuum cleaner was invented in 1902. Robot cleaners are now being developed. They have a memory so that they can remember a route round a room, without knocking into obstacles.

Ingenious Inventions

Wheel power
How did early humans come up with the idea of making the wheel? To move heavy objects, people would roll them on tree trunks

Patenting inventions
If you invent something, you want to make sure that no one copies it. Patents can be bought to establish this.
Patenting goes back to times when royalty granted trading rights to favourites.

Fire alarm
When early humans discovered fire, how did they put it out? Fire extinguishers were not invented until 1816.

High jumps
The first parachute was made and used in Paris in 1797. A Russian woman holds the female record for parachuting, having made over 8,000 jumps.

Printing a page
Who invented a printing press, so that books like this one could be made? The earliest printed book was made in China in AD868. In Germany in 1450 a printing press was invented by Gutenberg.

Phoning home
In 1876, Alexander Bell invented something that would change modern communications – the telephone. A receiver and transmitter are connected by an electrical current.

Robot world
People have been interested in robots for a long time. The Ancient Greeks even had a brass robot in their myths. Modern robots have been invented to do some of the tasks that humans find dull.

Royalty and Rulers

Long live leaves
The Zulu King Cetshwayo was forced to go to London to meet Queen Victoria in 1879. He nobly defied the Queen by wearing traditional clothes.

Reigning royals

The longest reigning King in the world was probably Phiops II in ancient Egypt. His reign began at six years of age and is thought to have continued until he was around one hundred years old.

King Mswati III of Swaziland, born in 1968, is the world's youngest king.

The shortest reign in history must be claimed for the son of King Dom Luis III, who was shot dead. His son was also shot but lived on for about 20 minutes. So it could be said that as King Dom Luis was dead, his son and heir became king for his dying half hour.

Long trek
Czar Paul I of Russia was inspecting his troops one day in 1798. He became annoyed when he noticed that one of his soldier's buttons was not polished. He ordered all 4,000 soldiers to march to Siberia. They set off, and were never heard of again.

Country claims
King Henry II of England, decided that he wanted to rule Ireland in 1155. He took it over claiming that the Pope had agreed to it. The people of Ireland had no say.

Crowning glories
The wearing of crowns can be traced back at least 5,000 years. They may have first been used as fancy headbands, to help keep the ruler's hair out of his or her eyes.

Warfare

Friendly football
During the First World War some German and British soldiers stopped fighting and played football one Christmas.

The longest siege
The longest siege recorded in history was at Ashdod in Israel. The siege lasted for nearly 30 years, from 664BC.

Shooting stars
Guns are constantly being developed to be faster and more accurate. In the USA a gun fired an object up to a height of 180km.

The children's crusade
The Christian crusades were filled with excessive bloodshed in their fight to regain the Holy Land. Hundreds of young children set sail from France to fight the Muslims in a children's crusade to the Holy Land. They never got the chance. Their ship was captured and they were sold as slaves.

Battle cries
In olden times it was important for leaders to be able to cry out loudly to their soldiers. The normal range at which the human voice can be heard clearly and understood is about 180m.

War and Peace

Early days
As far back as 200,000 BC, people made weapons. In those times they made wooden spears. Such primitive weapons could be used to kill a person.

The big bang
In 1945 the first atomic bomb was used. Unlike the wooden spear, this weapon killed not one, but nearly 100,000 people. A single nuclear submarine now has the firepower which is eight times that used in World War II.

The cost of war
The governments of the world direct an increasing amount of their funds to military spending — over $1 million every minute. The amount spent in eight hours could rid the world's 200 million malaria sufferers of the disease.

Superstitions

Hot cross buns
Hot cross buns were originally baked and eaten on Good Friday. The buns were believed to have magical powers, including driving the devil away.

Sorcery and Superstition

Lucky charms
Superstitions are beliefs that have sometimes developed over many years from witchcraft and sorcery. You may have created a superstition of your own, by having an object or charm that you consider to be lucky.

Silly superstitions
Over time, many superstitions have lost their original meaning. Some do have sensible as well as superstitious origins. If you walk under a ladder, something could easily fall on your head from above. Other superstitions may have completely lost their meaning now.

Lucky find
Finding a four-leafed clover is said to bring good fortune. They can be kept as a lucky charm.

Watch your step!
Walking under a ladder means a blow of fate will occur. It is unlucky to step on the odd rungs of a ladder.

Mirror, mirror on the wall...
There are many superstitions attached to mirrors. To avoid seven years bad luck on breaking a mirror, touch wood, or spit on the broken pieces of the mirror.

Touch wood
In ancient times, people believed that magical gods lived in trees. By touching a tree trunk you could gain some magical powers.

Myths and Legends

Merry Christmas
Christmas was previously a pagan Roman festival. The Christians then decided to make it their festival.

Atlantic notion
Atlantis was said to be a huge, beautiful island, situated in the Atlantic Ocean. If it ever existed, where did it go? It is thought that as a result of earthquakes, the island of Atlantis and all its people were swallowed up by the sea.

Double trouble
In Roman myths, Romulus and Remus were abandoned baby twins. They were mothered by a wolf and survived. Romulus later killed Remus.

Lucky birds
By law, the Tower of London keeps a minimum of six well-fed ravens. In the reign of Charles II it was said that if all ravens left the tower, disaster would strike.

Waltzing Matilda
In this Australian song, the ghost of a bush tramp is said to be heard by anyone walking past a particular billabong. A billabong is a dried-up waterhole, which the tramp jumped into after sheep stealing.

Old Tales

Myths and legends can be modern or ancient. Perhaps the best are the ones that have been passed down from generation to generation. But what is a myth? It is a story that has come from the imagination. Legends come from elaborations of history.

Since ancient times
Many ancient myths were told by the Greeks and Romans. These civilised peoples used their imaginations to great effect. They used their stories of extraordinary gods to explain the inexplicable. Most cultures have created stories from their imaginations to explain life.

Northern tales
In Scandinavia, the Norse people created many tales. They were passed on by word of mouth. The stories would often be made into long poems, so that they were easier to remember. Many tales from all cultures have a moral to tell, which acts as a way to guide people's behaviour.

Facts and Fallacies

Aesop's fables
There is a famous book of moral tales, named after a man called Aesop, who was born a Greek slave. However, no one really knows if these animal tales were his stories.

Nasty Nero
Nero was a rather uncaring Roman Emperor. When a massive fire raged through Rome for nine days, it was said that he sat in his bath ignoring it.

St Patrick prays
Saint Patrick is said to have created a miracle in France. He prayed for food and a herd of wild pigs appeared.

A wild goose chase
Who was Mother Goose, with whom so many children's stories are linked? It appears that she was not a goose at all, but Queen Goosefoot, the mother of the French King Charlemagne.

True or False

An exact fact?
What exactly is a fact? It is a description of something that has actually happened or a piece of knowledge that can be proved to be true.

Then what is a fallacy? It is an idea that you may believe is true but is false, because it is based on information that is wrong, or a faulty way of reasoning something out.

False facts
How can you tell the difference between a fact and a fallacy? For instance, some events in the past are very difficult to prove. You have to look at all the information you can find and make up your own mind.

The dashing Sir Drake
Sir Francis Drake was an English Admiral. He was said to be a great gentleman and to have laid down his cloak over a puddle to stop Queen Elizabeth from getting her feet wet.

Index

A
aeroplanes, 10, 12
Aesop, 30
Atlantis, 28

B
babies, 5
bank, 19
bank notes, 18, 19
barter, 8

C
cheques, 19
children, 5
Chinese, 5, 14, 15
Christmas, 28
cities, 4
clover, 26
crowns, 23
crusade, 25
coins, 18

D
dentist, 7
devil, 8, 26
Drake, Sir Francis, 31

E
Edison, Thomas, 20

F
fakirs, 11
First World War, 24
flame thrower, 13

G
growth, 7
guns, 24

H
hair, 6
heart, 7

I
Ireland, 23

L
ladder, 26, 27
languages, 14, 15

M
maggots, 12
mice, 9, 16
mirrors, 27
monk, 10
mother goose, 31
mountaineering, 11

N
necks, 7
Nero, Emperor, 30

O
olive eating, 11
orator, 15

P
parachuting, 21
patents, 21
pies, 17
population, 4
post, 9, 14
printing, 21

R
ravens, 29
restaurant, 12
Romulus and Remus, 28

S
sailing, 12
Saint Patrick, 30
Sandwich, Earl of, 17
siege, 24
Spartans, 9

T
tax, 18
telephones, 14, 21
television, 14
truffles, 16

V
vacuum cleaner, 20

W
walking, 10, 11
Waltzing Matilda, 29
water, 6, 7
weaponry, 25
whale, 12
wheel, 20
wood, 27
writer, 12

The publisher has made every effort to trace ownership of all copyrighted illustrations and to secure permission for their reproduction. In the event of any question arising as to the use of such material the publisher, whilst expressing regret for inadvertent error will be pleased to make the necessary corrections in future printings.